Yankee Modern

YANKEE MODERN

The Houses of Estes/Twombly

William Morgan

PRINCETON ARCHITECTURAL PRESS, NEW YORK

Published by
Princeton Architectural Press
37 East 7th Street, New York, NY 10003

For a free catalog of books, call 1-800-722-6657
Visit our website at www.papress.com

Editor: Lauren Nelson Packard
Designer: Paul Wagner

Special thanks to: Nettie Aljian, Bree Anne Apperley, Sara Bader,
Nicola Bednarek, Janet Behning, Becca Casbon, Carina Cha,
Penny (Yuen Pik) Chu, Carolyn Deuschel, Russell Fernandez,
Pete Fitzpatrick, Wendy Fuller, Jan Haux, Clare Jacobson, Aileen Kwun,
Nancy Eklund Later, Linda Lee, Laurie Manfra, John Myers, Katharine Myers,
Dan Simon, Andrew Stepanian, Jennifer Thompson, Joseph Weston,
and Deb Wood of Princeton Architectural Press
—Kevin C. Lippert, publisher

Library of Congress Cataloging-in-Publication Data
Morgan, William, 1944–
Yankee modern : the houses of Estes/Twombly / William Morgan. — 1st ed.
    p.   cm.
ISBN 978-1-56898-817-7 (alk. paper)
1. Estes/Twombly. 2. Architecture, Domestic—
New England. I. Title. II. Title: Houses of Estes/Twombly.
NA7239.E88A4 2009
728.0974—dc22
                                        2009006733

pages 2–3:
Danevic/Barker House; Barker House Garage

Foreword

Howard Mansfield

Newport, Rhode Island, lures millions of visitors to its Gilded Age mansions, so it is perhaps an odd place for architects to be practicing the art of what might be called the un-Mansion. Here, a few blocks from the swarming tourists, Jim Estes and Peter Twombly design trim houses that recall another Newport tradition, sailing. In their houses, as in yachts, there is no wasted gesture. Sailboats don't pretend to be anything but what they are, and the same is true of the houses of Estes/Twombly. "I don't like to lay on a lot of trim and decoration. Natural materials should speak for themselves," says Estes. And Twombly adds, "A lot of it is keeping things simple and common sense."

Their houses are modest and the materials are familiar—shingles weathered gray, white-painted trim. The results are liberating. With oversized windows and open interiors, their houses seem to float. The second floor of the Osprey House is one big room, lined with windows. The house faces the East Passage of Narragansett Bay, and to live in that room is to have a harbor master's command. The third floor of a recent project, a renovated Victorian, has been opened up to one room that looks across the water to Newport.

It's another lookout that invites lingering.

But what is most pleasing about their houses is their intelligence. The designs are fresh; the houses are awake. Nothing is done here by rote, whether it is modern or traditional. The houses are like a conversation rejoined, a conversation about building within a tradition in a way that is true to the times. Each design is an honest answer to the old question: What is a house?

Answering this simple question is an American obsession. Each era has had its excesses and reformers, whether it's Thoreau making a statement with his cabin at Walden Pond, A. J. Downing attacking the plague of "glaring white" houses, Edith Wharton attacking the plague of "hideous" New York brownstones, or Catharine Beecher preaching ethical homemaking. This is only a short dip in the genre of Thy Neighbor's House (and Why It's Wrong). Our own era has given us the bloated McMansion and a fever of TV shows seeking to Flip *This* House/Flip *That* House and redecorate in ten minutes for ten dollars. And it has given us serious reformers as well, whether it's architects trying to apply Christopher

page 8:
Living room, Horgan Cottage

opposite:
Horgan Cottage, Jamestown, RI

following spread:
Farm outbuildings, Little Compton, RI

Alexander's Pattern Language, or to build environmentally ethical houses, to mention only two trends.

Jim Estes and Peter Twombly lay out no manifesto. They are not pulpit thumpers. They don't lecture; they don't teach. Their answer is to design good small houses that are memorable. "Good houses burn an image in your mind," says Estes. Photographed at twilight, their houses are beckoning. They prove what Gaston Bachelard said in *The Poetics of Space*: "The lamp in the window is the house's eye." The house at twilight "sees, keeps vigil, and vigilantly waits." Home waits for us. The Estes/Twombly houses do another simple thing well: they look like home.

These welcoming images have been popping up on different blogs lately, being shared with enthusiasm. "I'm having a little thing for Estes/Twombly right now," a blogger in the Pacific Northwest writes about her "new crush." "I like how they think. Simple, straightforward, and with attention to the space around the structure…it's lovely. Okay, more than lovely. This is like twilight house eye candy bliss. That term won't be sweeping the nation anytime soon, but it's how I feel."

This fanzine talk would embarrass the modest Estes and Twombly, who have a touch of Yankee reticence, but it shows that in this era of the Too-Big House and the Too-Big Mortgage, there is a hunger for small, beautiful houses.

From the city that taught Americans how to live large, here are ten houses—un-Mansions—set against the tide of the McMansion.

Yankee Modern

William Morgan

A small house on an island. This understated domestic work—modest, unassuming, covered in shingles—illustrates the philosophy of architects James Estes and Peter Twombly.

Constructed of local materials among the stone walls and open fields of Block Island, this square, two-story cottage respectfully blends in among its farmhouse neighbors. This is intentional, for the architects who began their building careers as carpenters believe that the best work can be innovative, but it must always be simple. Theirs is a quiet modernism built upon the traditional and the familiar.

Such regionally appropriate design does not dazzle or shout, but is refreshingly clean and decisive when compared to the overblown pastiche-laden evocations of the Shingle Style and the Colonial Revival that crowd the New England shore. Even so, the little house is not without stylistic references. The peaked gable on the south facade echoes those adorning many nineteenth-century cottages on Block Island. The source of this decorative element was the popular pattern books of Andrew Jackson Downing, the guru of the well-designed house for the common man in

the late nineteenth century. Scroll-sawn decoration adorned many of Downing's patterns, yet homebuilders all across the country simply added the peaked gable to their plain boxes and dispensed with the more expensive Carpenter's Gothic trim. Plus here the exposed maritime landscape demanded a forthright and frugal architecture.

A no-nonsense farmhouse aesthetic infuses the Block Island house. Windows are standard millwork, two-over-two double-hung sash. The tool shed is connected to the house by a metal track carrying a sliding barn door which can be pulled across to protect the entry terrace from the island's bitter winds (this is a year-round house in an often brutal climate) and create an outdoor room. The shed itself looks like most other utilitarian add-ons, but its role in defining and protecting the outdoor space is equally important as its role for storing tools.

Yet the house should not be seen merely as the domestic equivalent of sensible denim overalls. The windows abutting each other at the corner of the house—a characteristic Estes/Twombly detail—express the tautness of the white cedar skin and dematerialize the sense of wall. Inside, a galvanized steel beam allows an open, light-filled plan and sets the tone for other galvanized, utilitarian hardware and detailing such as the diamond plate steel hearth for the wood stove.

The owners wanted a house that was inexpensive to build and maintain, and this is the smallest house the architects have ever done. This felicitous and handsome combination of modernity and thrift is one of the firm's most published works. Its simplicity and directness is especially apparent when compared with Block Island's famous modern composition, a house and studio built by Robert Venturi thirty years ago. While the revolutionary father of Post-Modernism employed the basic materials and forms of the island, he was making intellectual references to historical architecture that was definitely "off island." For example, in building one of his "decorated sheds" he employed an emphatic signifier, a Roman bath window with a genealogy stretching from the Emperor Constantine to Thomas Jefferson. The Estes/Twombly house is, less self-consciously, an undecorated shed.

In the time that separates Venturi's small shingled compositions from those of Twombly and Estes, the younger architects rediscovered, even resuscitated, a truer spirit of the practical yet quietly elegant coastal New England house. Venturi may have reignited an appreciation of the simple shingled aesthetic with two 1970 houses on Nantucket. But, as with so much Post-Modernism, those houses and those by Venturi's followers were preoccupied with details and appearances. Yale historian Vincent Scully called Venturi's Nantucket houses true vernacular architecture— common, buildable, traditional in the deepest sense, and of piercing symbolic power. But the description more accurately describes Estes/Twombly's Block Island cottage of thirty years later. That house recaptured the ethic of an iconic regional house type—a way of building, as well as an understanding of what a house in this place needs to be.

That time span also represents Estes and Twombly's education, years of practice, and exploration toward their distinctive voice. Both principals received their architectural training at the Rhode Island School of Design, but their routes there differed.

Raised in suburban Boston, with summer vacations in New Hampshire and on Cape Cod, Twombly decided on an architectural career as a young boy and went straight into the architecture program at RISD. During school breaks he was a carpenter. He worked several years with Michael Graves in Princeton (where he was the project architect for the Newark Museum). Following a stint with Rafael Viñoly in New York and a couple of years in Iowa City with Hanson Lind Meyer, a landlocked Twombly returned to New England and established his own firm in Providence. The like-minded architects were part of the Providence architectural scene, where both admired and respected each other's work. They joined forces in Newport, and in 2000 they incorporated as Estes/Twombly. Both architects live on Conanicut Island, where, when work permits, Twombly does some lobstering and Estes builds stone walls.

Jim Estes' journey to the six-person Newport firm was a bit more circuitous, although it too involved a bit of rambling around New England. After graduating from Darmouth College with an English major, Estes discovered architecture working as a carpenter for David Sellers in Vermont. Sellers' radical group of mostly Yale-trained artists and architects emphasized the art of building and working with nature, long before those ideas became fashionable—or rather a hundred years after they went out of fashion. Following graduation from the Rhode Island School of Design, Estes designed and built houses, sometimes working alone and sometimes in other offices. For a decade he practiced architecture with William Burgin, another RISD graduate.

Burgin and Estes did well designing large houses around Newport and in Jamestown, its more modest neighbor across the bay. The Rhode Island colonial capital's rich architectural legacy runs from Georgian through Victorian, as well as the panoply of styles chosen for the mansions of the very rich at the turn of the twentieth century. So it is not surprising that the young architects whipped up houses in French Provincial, Queen Anne, and Stick Style, although many designs favored that uniquely New England seaside expression called the Shingle Style.

One such house, built in a neighborhood of shingled cottages in Jamestown and enjoying a spectacular prospect of the bridge over to Newport, expresses this period in Estes' career. It does not pretend to be a plate from Scully's eponymous book on the Shingle Style, but it shares the best characteristic of the style: mixed materials, with cedar shingles above a rough masonry foundation, an asymmetrical skyline featuring an exaggerated saltbox form, and a picturesque gaggle of porches, dormers, and windows to take in the view joining outdoors and indoors.

The house won some awards and was published in some magazines and a book. This publicity elicited a somewhat alarming phone call from a man who wanted to buy the plans and build a version of the house on a bluff outside of Wichita. What made the house belong in Rhode Island and not Kansas? Estes wondered. The layout and materials were pretty standard, and the heating and cooling system could handle prairie summers as well as New England winters. Yet, the house was designed as a continuation of local traditions, and its success was predicated on its response to the site. If the architect was doing his job well, the house should be totally inappropriate.

Estes' musings about time and place coincided with the large, style-driven houses across the country, notably in places along the shore, where they were totally unsuited. This was especially the case in eastern Long Island, which in the 1950s and 60s was a laboratory for New York architects fashioning contemporary weekend houses that nestled into the rugged landscape of sand dunes and pine scrub. Pre-air conditioning, these modest designs used natural materials that required little maintenance and were carefully placed to take advantage of sun and breezes. In contrast, their large and ornate successors that marched across the landscapes of the Hamptons and Cape Cod were an insult to both the environment and common sense.

Clients approached Estes/Twombly wanting retro houses that recalled simpler times while providing a warmth and charm they felt lacking in modernism. While decrying the generic similarity of most new American housing, as well as the absurdity of increasingly larger houses, the architects sought to pursue clients who would appreciate smaller houses that responded to their surroundings. "We wanted to do a regional architecture that went beyond variations on style, and that would become a synthesis of local influences resulting in buildings that were unique to their time and place."

Beginning with the little house on Block Island in 1999, the Estes/Twombly firm focused on responsibly sized dwellings and common sense solutions to issues of style and climate. "Toward a smaller house" may not have the clarion ring of a revolutionary manifesto, yet this notion is based on deeply held philosophical principles. The houses in this book range from 1,000 to 3,200 square feet.

In using basic New England forms and materials as a language for new compositions, the architects attempt to distill traditional architecture to its basic forms. The Wolf House in Warwick, for example, employs an almost childlike schema of gable, shed, and chimney to create a compelling image that says "house." In addition to the straightforward use of prototypical forms, the materials—shingles, standing seam metal roof, and stucco—are equally common, yet the skillful juxtaposing of one against the other brings out their nature. The architects use all these elements in a fresh way that avoids a confection of past details.

Equally important, the designers strive to reveal a sense of place through their architecture. The typical new American home relies on a shell that defies local conditions and is a greedy consumer of energy. Estes and Twombly's approach, however, obviates the need for mechanical heating and cooling systems by creating such passive design elements as overhangs and ventilation patterns.

Estes' own home in Jamestown, for example, has a closed north face while the south front is open with pronounced overhangs calculated to keep out the summer sun while letting in lower cast winter light. High windows under the eaves can be left open all summer to take advantage of breezes. Just as with the small house on Block Island, where barn doors close to create a sheltered outdoor space, here the entire house acts as a windbreak.

The architect's house is sheathed in barn siding made from selectively cut and locally milled eastern white pine. Clapboards of rough pine are a respectful nod to a couple of centuries of regional houses and barns, and by extension acknowledge a sense of place. By using locally available materials, the architects reacquaint us with what has worked in the past and how generations of builders have dealt with the local weather. While their work is contemporary, the architects rely on simple, time-tested approaches to home building.

Appreciation and elevation of the ordinary is also reflected in the Estes and Twombly approach to details. Rather than straining to be clever and original, they discover new qualities in everyday things, thus revealing the inherent beauty of an object or a material through explicit and direct detailing. Colanders used as light sconces transform an everyday kitchen tool into a new utility (in a Duchampian way, we are challenged to see the mundane as a work of art). The redefinition of objects, such as the colander, through different uses or treatments is a common thread in Estes/Twombly's work; in another project for a toy manufacturer they used corrugated steel silo sections as desk bases and room dividers. Placing rough stone work next to a smooth slab of cherry, or exposing an old brick chimney and highlighting it by placing it adjacent to a beaded wood cabinet, are examples of letting the materials speak for themselves and revealing their character. All of the interior hardware for the small Block Island house is available in the Stanley hardware catalog, reminding us that good design is not necessarily a function of high cost.

Such straightforward Modernist detailing—of achieving richness through economy—sets aside the houses of Etstes/Twombly from the typically grander estates blossoming along the New England coast. While the smaller, more sensitive houses make for a diminished carbon footprint, they also make for less fanfare. For the architects, a house should not shout for attention, and the more understated it can be the better. But these houses are harder to design, like writing a sonnet or a haiku within the discipline imposed by the formal structure. So, in spite of responding to very local influences, Estes/Twombly's work has achieved universality, not unlike such successful long running house types as the Cape Cod cottage or the traditional Japanese farmhouse.

Even so, each Estes/Twombly house is for a specific place and client, and part of their impact is that each is special. While they may be builders at heart, Jim and Peter are architects, creating works of art that are best measured against other one-off designs. Architects they admire include Lake/Flato, Rick Joy, Peter Bohlin, and James Cutler, all of whom are known for regionally appropriate design. It would make no more sense to put a Rhode Island house by Estes and Twombly in the Arizona desert than it would to put one of Rick Joy's southwestern desert houses in Newport.

Consider Windshield, the more overtly Modern house that Richard Neutra built on Fishers Island in 1938. Just two years after Frank Lloyd Wright's iconic Fallingwater, Neutra's sleek, flat-roofed composition with America's first aluminum sash was a major work of the European international style as filtered by years of practice in Los Angeles. While the destruction of this major monument by fire in 1973 was a tragedy, its severe modernism—Neutra's claim to be a "modernist regionalist" to the contrary—can hardly be seen as a harbinger of a new northeastern style.

With backgrounds in construction, Jim Estes and Peter Twombly have approached architecture through the act of building. Their details and shapes often derive from a knowledge of materials and how they

are best joined. Their reaction to a site stems from their familiarity with the land and spending time outdoors. This is not purely academic or classroom learning but is a more pragmatic search for the universality of the local. Boston architect Peter Rose aptly described this search for linking between buildings and land and between buildings and people:

> Almost every farm building or cluster of farm buildings I ever saw seemed so firmly embedded in climate, topography and landscape that I began to think that if farmers can do it, and if mediocre architects in the nineteenth century could do it, there was something that they were doing. My sense was that they were simply taking more time and smelling and listening and looking and coming back at night and coming back in winter and just getting a feel for the place.

Can these ten houses and the others done by Jim Estes and Peter Twombly really change how we perceive and design our homes? Humble and modest are not characteristics that come to mind when describing the architecture of the early twenty-first century, yet humility and modesty are the end products, if not the stated goals, of the Estes/Twombly firm. Architects design only two percent of new homes built in this country, and many of those who avail themselves of design services want a home that suggests a certain bygone grandeur. In contrast, by responding to local conditions and using inexpensive and readily available materials, these houses form a template for a regional style that works both practically and spiritually; they make economic sense and are environmentally responsible. In their quiet way, the architects have created fertile ground for the union of the traditional and the contemporary in New England's rocky soil.

Wolf House

The village of Potowomut on Greenwich Bay is typically Rhode Island, but in a different way than, say, Block Island or Newport. A century ago, most Rhode Islanders who spent summers at the shore stayed in colonies of modest weekend cottages. Many of these oceanfront communities are now inhabited year round. The Wolf House is part of a neighborhood of cottages that have been winterized. The owner grew up here, moved back from a career in New York, and wanted a house that fit in with the neighbors.

The L-shaped plan reads like one of Frank Lloyd Wright's classic Usonian houses: continuously flowing living space wraps around and forms a private terraced courtyard (the lot is only one hundred by one hundred feet). A third-story painting studio creates a picturesque vertical focal point, which is one of three individual and distinctly separate workspaces for each member of the family.

The house is richly detailed and responds to the context of New England without resorting to clichés and applied decoration. Its exterior shapes, materials, and details are traditional; most forms are simple gable boxes that extend to the ground. Windows are basic two-over-two punched into the shingle skin.

Inside, materials, forms, and details are even further simplified. The basic house shapes are apparent on the interiors and in place of moldings and paneling, different cabinets and surfaces are defined by different materials in a simple, unadorned state. Plaster walls have subtle color variations to define different planes. These colors also link spaces that bleed into each other, such as the hallway and stairway.

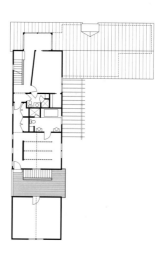

Third floor

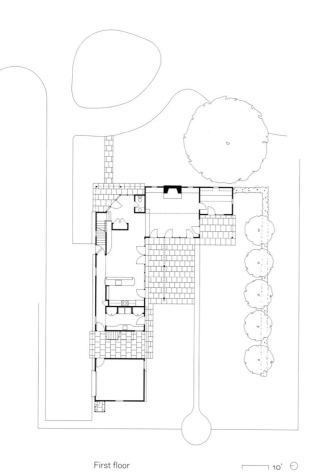

First floor

⊏———⊐ 10' ⊖

Second floor

Cyronak House

Shortly after the Cyronak House was built, a prominent businessman came to the architects to talk about doing a large Shingle Style house on the shore. He looked at a photograph of this house and expressed surprise at why such a home would need an architect. This unintended compliment gets to the heart of the complexity of the simple.

The clients were decidedly in tune with the Block Island aesthetic and wanted a house that would capture the directness of the island's older buildings. They also understood that the best materials were those that had already proven to be easy to maintain and able to withstand many months of bad weather. Their home is attuned to many seasons, where activities overflow to the deck and terrace in the summertime, and outdoor living is extended into the fall and spring by closing sliding barn doors to block off the wind. In the winter the house proper becomes a more contained safe haven.

Of all the images of this much-photographed house, that of the shower enclosure best epitomizes the philosophy of the utilitarian. The straightforward detailing of common materials to fulfill a need can transcend the utilitarian and become beautiful. Corrugated plastic is used for the enclosure. It not only makes reference to galvanized steel of New England farm buildings, but it is a practical, inexpensive response to the need for an outdoor space to wash up after a day at the beach. It also captures the essence of summer on Block Island, in much the same way as screen doors slamming, laundry flapping on a clothesline, and round beach stones serving as doorstops.

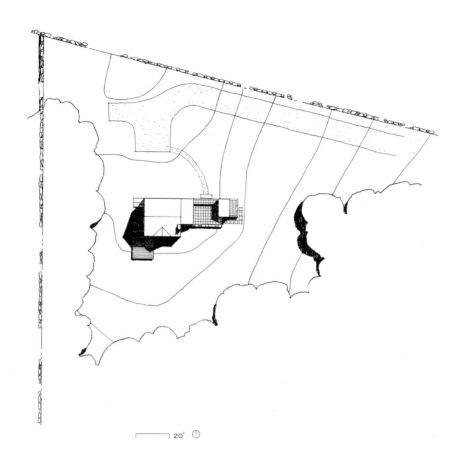

CYRONAK HOUSE

40

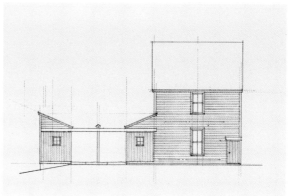

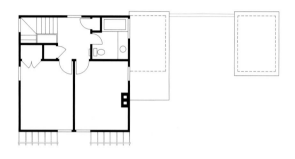

Second floor

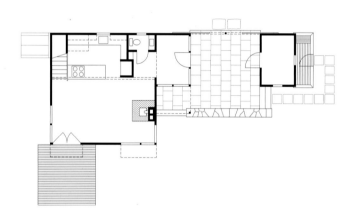

First floor

 10'

Freeman House

The house overlooks Bristol Harbor, one of colonial New England's thriving ports. It draws inspiration from two well-known nineteenth-century resort styles: the roughhewn Adirondack camp and the elegant yet casual shingled cottage. This summer getaway designed for an extended family is like a treasured photograph album that embodies memories of generations of vacations.

The plan clearly delineates public and private functions, sleeping wing and living area. A two-story bunkhouse, angled to one side of the living/dining/kitchen space, is a straightforward gable-roofed block with two-over-two windows. In contrast to the practical bunkhouse, the main living space is open to the rafters with a massive floor-to-ceiling stone fireplace. This giant hearth anchors the expansively glazed common space. Stone steps lead to a loft above the dining room.

The contrast of solidity and openness—of exposed and sheltered spaces—pervades the house's program. Rooms and decks are bright and airy on the waterside, whereas on the landside the rooms are smaller, more introverted. The landscape reflects this as well. A stone wall and a grove of birches are part of the intimately scaled path that leads from the driveway to the house. A small terrace with a pergola connects the entry walk with the study.

The view from the front door offers a glimpse of the harbor. Views of the water expand as one moves farther into the house. The visual journey toward the water culminates in large open decks. The porch wraps around two sides of the house and brings living areas outside. Overhanging eaves block the summer sun and provide a sheltered outdoor space in off seasons. The patriarchal chimney extends onto the deck, which has a fireplace for grilling and offers an ideal family gathering point.

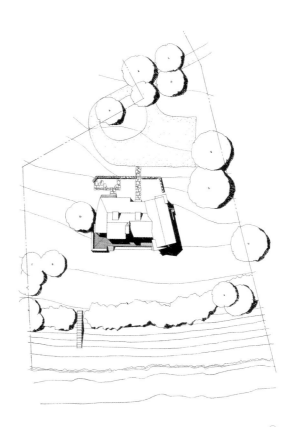

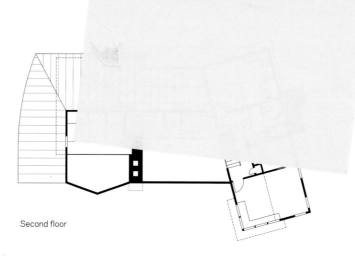

Second floor

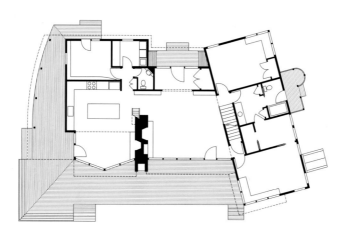

First floor

|————————| 10'

Estes House

The rusted remnants of a giant boiler rise like an abstract sculpture, standing sentinel over what was an extensive flower-growing complex. The skeletal end of the main greenhouse defines the back end of the four-acre site. These were left as reminders of the place's commercial history. In keeping with this history, the long low profile of the house is reminiscent of the original two-hundred-foot glass building.

Once cleared of a half century of neglect, this remarkable in-town property offered meadow, wetlands, and a surrounding buffer of woods, all of which was preserved by siting the house at the north corner of the lot. The house's lightly fenestrated north facade functions as a wall separating the public, suburban side of the site from the private wetland side. The center of the L-shaped plan has a thirty-eight by twenty-one-foot living/dining/kitchen space beneath exposed rafters. A pergola continues beyond the living room at the west end, further delineating public and private realms. On the east, the axis turns ninety degrees at the master bedroom and leads to a two-story wing that contains a garage and a small apartment. Each wing has a tower, which adds to the agricultural spirit of the domestic composition. The roofing is barnyard grade galvanized steel. The siding is rough sawn eastern white pine, like that used on New England barns.

A ten-foot-wide bluestone sidewalk passes through the house from the main entry, across the dining room and out to the family terrace. Unlike the north side's small clerestory windows, the south side has a wall of glass doors that extends the living space outside. There is no air conditioning because wide eaves cut out the summer sun, allowing windows to be left open in most weather; the whole house is like a nineteenth-century sleeping porch. With the twelve-foot doors open at night, one can hear the sounds of wildlife in the woods and the buoy bells on Narragansett Bay.

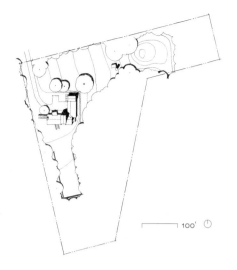

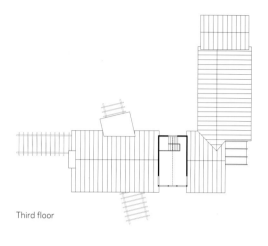

Third floor

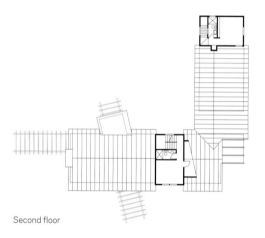

Second floor

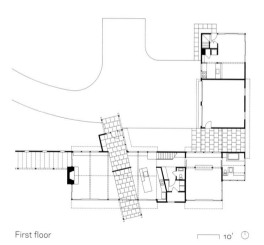

First floor

100'

10'

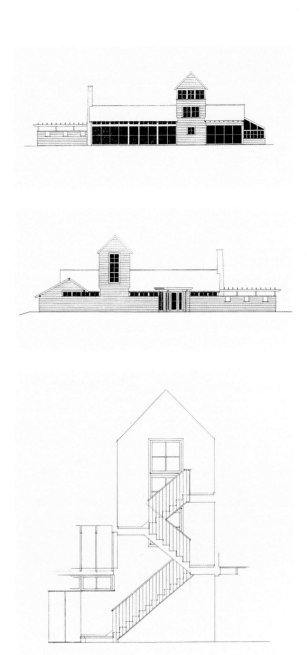

O'Leary House

The genesis of this design was the challenge posed by an awkwardly shaped strip of land: there was a ninety-five-foot waterfront, but the lot was six hundred feet deep. A couple of old stone breakwaters defined and protected a small private beach. These served as inspiration for the idea of two separate buildings running nearly parallel with the lot. Instead of planting a house perpendicular to the water, the architects defined views and shielded family life from neighbors by echoing the breakwater configuration.

Gabled ends of the house and the garage/studio wing form the unassuming public face of the compound. The two buildings are connected by a sliding barn door that can be opened to provide a glimpse of the water or closed to block cool winds. The buildings are angled so that the courtyard space between the wings widens toward the water. By manipulating the perspective in this way, the southeastern views open up with space seemingly borrowed from the neighboring lots. Because of this careful placement, all of the rooms have water views, and all living spaces are oriented to the expanding, south-facing courtyard.

At the front, rectangular sheds are anchored by a common low facade, which is clad in flush cedar boarding and painted an earthy red in contrast to the weathered gray shingles above. Differentiating the floors in this way visually grounds the house and mitigates the building's increasing height as the ground slopes down towards the beach.

The modest program called for a living room connected to a kitchen and dining room, a study, a studio, and three bedrooms. Interior finishes are kept light and all the trim and exposed framing is painted white, creating rich shadows in the sun drenched interior. Stock cabinets and stair parts were used to save on costs. Such economies reveal reliance on good proportions and craftsmanship rather than on decoration or extravagance.

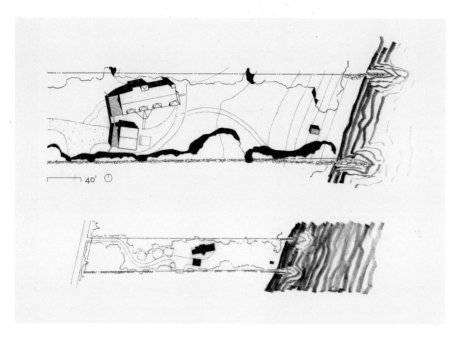

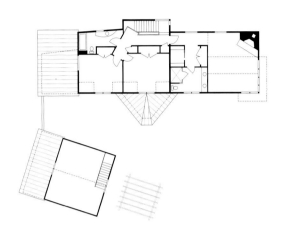

Second floor

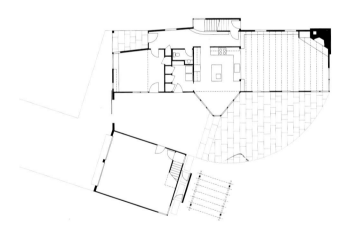

First floor

 10'

McKeough House

This summer cottage, with its porches, Block Island dormers, and wood shingles, appears to be one of the firm's more eclectic houses. The Philadelphia clients did, in fact, want a strictly traditional house, and they came to an initial conversation bearing pictures of island houses they liked. There was a common thread running through their simply detailed and well-proportioned examples. All employed the peaked dormer, as well as the typical local porch arrangement of an attached hipped roof shed.

These forms and details served as a starting point, but they were employed in unusual ways. The Block Island dormer was their basic unit, but it has been refined, making it almost archetypal in form—like something a child might draw, a straight-forward yet elegant image expressing "house." A more sophisticated domestic composition was achieved by playing with these Monopoly-like house units in a variety of combinations. Despite appearances,

the result is a strikingly modern house, wearing its patrimony lightly.

Three dormers present the house's face, viewed from across an open meadow. These picturesque peaked elements are divided, two to one side and one to another. Both separating and thematically joining them is an entry porch covered by a low-pitched shed roof. The porch flows inside to become a large open living space. Then it continues through the house, where it becomes a platform from which to con-template the open Atlantic. The structure of the porch is expressed in the living room's raised ceiling and exposed rafters. Dueling stairs lead up to each sleep-ing block from this central space.

Halls, bathrooms, and support spaces are lined up on the north side of the house, while most of the glazing faces the southern, ocean side. Being only one room deep, there are cross breezes and lots of light in all the rooms.

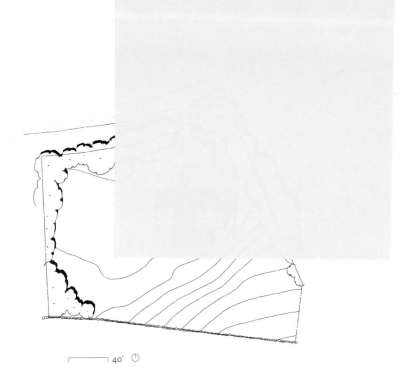

⊏——⊐ 40' ⊙

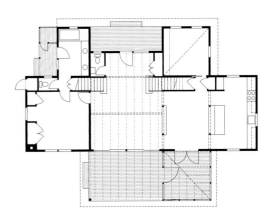

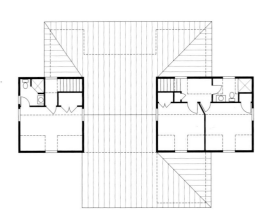

First floor   ⊏——⊐ 10' ⊙   Second floor

Osprey House

Osprey House stands where a fishing shack—often tossed off its pilings by hurricanes—once stood. The lot, a narrow strip of land between the water and the road, was presumably unbuildable. Setting the house on concrete stilts, however, addressed zoning and coastal setback restrictions. The foundations serve as sheltered open space that allows flood waters to pass underneath. Exposed galvanized structural supports complement the feeling of maritime utility. The metal roof is resistant to storm damage, while the white vinyl trim and aluminum-clad windows need little maintenance.

Given the small lot and its proximity to the road, service elements, along with small windows to help with cross ventilation, are grouped at the rear of the house. The entrance hall, two bedrooms, and a bathroom occupy the lower entry level. White walls, light maple floors, and pine trim add to the house's airiness and simplicity. The single-room living space on the second floor has windows on three sides, which take maximum advantage of the view of the bay, shipping lanes, and Newport on the opposite shore.

While this 1,440 square-foot vacation retreat maintains the humble workaday spirit of Jamestown's fishing shacks, the initial design proposed a more adventurous, less traditional roof shape than the standard double-pitch gable. But the zoning board rejected it on aesthetic grounds. In spite of the zoning board's intervention, this house is inherently modern in its spirit and intentions.

As with all of the houses featured in this book, regional context is a departure point for an exploration of contemporary domestic design. The simple configuration of the windows, for example, may recall those on New England farmhouses. But the openings here are placed right up to the corners of the house, accentuating the membrane-like quality of the shingled envelope and visually letting the house sit lightly on its concrete piers.

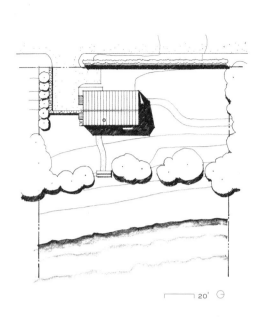

⌐━━━┐ 20' ⊖

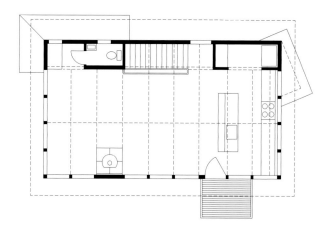

Second floor

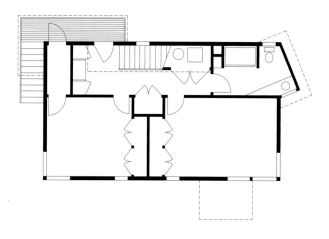

First floor

 10'

Barker House

Two business partners bought adjacent pieces of land on Block Island and each wanted a house. Although related by proximity, simultaneous conception, and the fact that their owners were friends, the houses are like fraternal twins: they have distinct personalities. Their common genes were the simple forms and rugged materials found in vernacular island architecture. And, each client wanted a viewing tower as well as second-floor living rooms.

This half of the pair of houses consists of three individual forms: baby gable, big gable, and rectangular tower, all connected in the nineteenth-century New England manner of organic accretions. The forms are arranged to create a sheltered place protected from the wind and rain and provide privacy for second floor indoor and outdoor living areas.

The garage (the baby gable) has large opposing barn doors so the workspace can be opened to the outside. A flat-roofed walkway joins the three forms, framing the entry and establishing a boundary between the public and private realms of the house (a corrugated plastic outdoor shower is on the lee side of the tower). The tower is clad in vertical white cedar boards while the rest of the house is covered in traditional shingles. The roof gables of the main living block are asymmetrical, a contemporary gesture that recalls the roof design for Osprey House.

Interior finishes are practical and minimal. The spare ruggedness of the landscape is brought indoors through extensive southern glazing and is reflected in the straightforward use of materials such as plywood ceilings and tongue-and-groove board paneling. The living space has small windows on the north side, and glass doors leading to an outside porch on the south, so the room offers protection from the elements while at the same time embracing the outdoors. The downstairs entry hall has white board walls, unadorned except for coat and hat pegs. The emotive power of this simple Shaker-like space is further graced by pure summer light from a narrow window on the stairs.

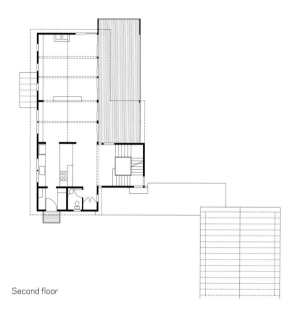

Second floor

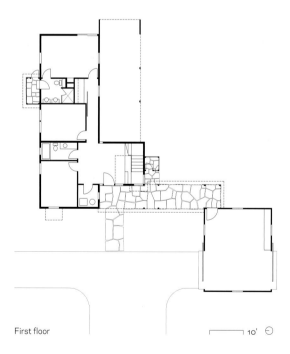

First floor

⌐———⌐ 10' ⊖

Danevic/Bernard House

Situated on two acres near the south shore of Block Island, this summer retreat for a couple and their two teenage sons is the complementary sibling of the shingled house built by friends next door. A tower serves as the fulcrum for a pair of two-story sheds, one of which contains a large open living space; the other houses guests and the boys. The plan allows half the house to be heated for occasional off-season weekends. The house turns its back to the north wind and the two blocks form a sun-catching courtyard.

The heart of the house is the single open living/dining/kitchen space on the second floor. Plywood cabinetry, exposed rafters, and views to the south and west contribute to a sense of lightness and informality. An open deck further joins inside and out, and provides a dining area and a belvedere from which to watch the sun set over Long Island Sound.

From the tower one can see the entire outline of Block Island, the coastlines of Connecticut, Rhode Island, and Massachusetts, as well as the lighthouse at Montauk Point on Long Island. It is the tower's form that captures the imagination. The ground floor is open, forming the entrance between arrival area and the inner court. Enclosed in a lattice, the second deck forms a bridge between living and sleeping wings. The top level crow's nest is open to the elements.

By day, the tower might be a secret lookout for kids playing; for adults seeking solitude high above the bustle of the house, it might become a refuge to catch up on summer reading, to knit, or to snooze. As a design element, the tower anchors and enlivens the horizontality of the house and recalls that most poetic example of seaside architecture, the lighthouse. By night, the tower undergoes a magical transformation and becomes a porous lantern, its daytime solidity giving way to the container of light from within.

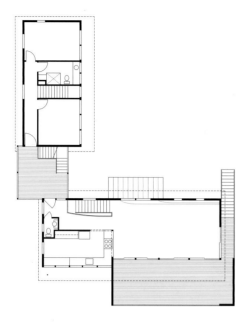

Second floor

First floor

⌐___⌐ 10' ⊖

Stonington House

Stonington is a well preserved nineteenth-century village complete with a notable collection of domestic architecture, tightly packed into a small peninsula that juts out into Long Island Sound. The surrounding countryside of stone walls and open fields is classic New England. The Stonington House—a cluster of small units in the big house-little house-back house-barn tradition—fits comfortably into this landscape of memory. But such appeal often brings unwelcome development, and the seven-acre mostly wetland site was rescued from developers by sensitive, caring clients.

The owners have lived in several interesting older houses, including an 1830s mill and a 1920s house with a chapel. But for this home they wanted something pared down and uncluttered as a backdrop for their collection of American folk art. Although the Stonington House is the largest of the ten houses, it maintains an intimate domestic scale.

Structures are limited to just a fraction of the property by wetland restrictions. Wanting to do the least amount of violence to the land, the architects used a gentle knoll as a plinth for the complex, and tied together the low-scaled group of barn, garage, living, and bedroom elements with walls of local granite. The plan also allows the creation of various sheltered outdoor spaces, while keeping masses low and avoiding a large boxy single building. The deliberately small lawn quickly gives way to grassy meadows and woods—home to turkeys, deer, and other wildlife. At the edge of the land is the ocean, visible from every room.

Characteristic Estes/Twombly metal roofing with deep overhangs protects the cedar shingle siding and painted trim. Within, the limited palate of materials and subdued colors serve as a quiet backdrop for paintings and ceramics. The open plan is equally simple, yet the diagonal juxtapositions of bedroom wing and utility buildings create a tension that subtly shapes each view of meadow or sea. An enormous stone hearth acts as a primeval anchor, balancing the sense of openness created by the large windows.

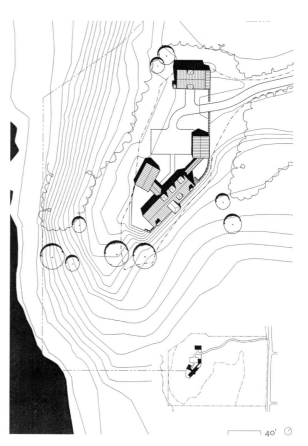

40'

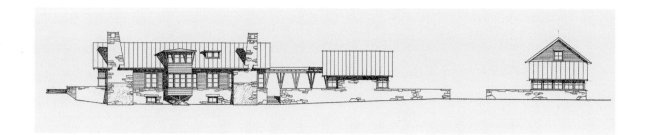

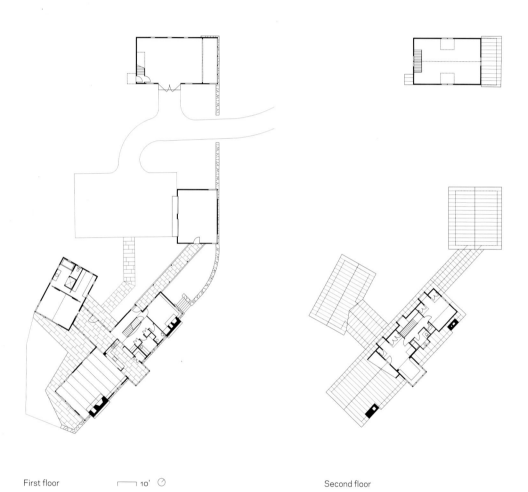

First floor   ⌐—⌐ 10' ⊘   Second floor

Project Credits

Wolf House (1998)
Location – Warwick, Rhode Island
Structural Engineer – Yoder & Tidwell, LTD,
    Providence, RI
Builder – Gardner Woodwrights, Saunderstown, RI
Photography – Warren Jagger, Providence, RI

Cyronak House (1999)
Location – Block Island, Rhode Island
Structural Engineer – Yoder & Tidwell, LTD,
    Providence, RI
Builder – John Spier, Block Island, RI
Photography – Warren Jagger, Providence, RI

Freeman House (2000)
Location – Bristol, Rhode Island
Structural Engineer – Yoder & Tidwell, LTD,
    Providence, RI
Landscape Architect – Martha Moore, Tiverton, RI
Builder – Highland Builders, Tiverton RI
Photography – Michael Mathers, Astoria, OR

Estes House (1999)
Location – Jamestown, Rhode Island
Structural Engineer – Yoder & Tidwell, LTD,
    Providence, RI
Builder – Walter Pilz, South Kingstown, RI
Photography – Michael Mathers, Astoria, OR, and
    Warren Jagger, Providence, RI

O'Leary House (2002)
Location – Jamestown, Rhode Island
Structural Engineer – Yoder & Tidwell, LTD,
    Providence, RI
Interiors – Estes/Twombly & Kirby Goff
Landscape – Thomas Succop, Pittsburgh, PA
Builder – Bruce Moniz, Newport, RI
Photography – Warren Jagger, Providence, RI

McKeough House (2003)
Location – Block Island, Rhode Island
Structural Engineer – Yoder & Tidwell, LTD,
   Providence, RI
Builder – McLaughlin & Buie Housewrights,
   E. Greenwich, RI
Photography – Warren Jagger, Providence, RI

Osprey House (2005)
Location – Jamestown, Rhode Island
Structural Engineer – Yoder & Tidwell, LTD,
   Providence, RI
Builder – Joseph Scotti, Jamestown, RI
Photography – Warren Jagger, Providence, RI

Barker House (2006)
Location – Block Island, Rhode Island
Structural Engineer – Yoder & Tidwell, LTD.,
   Providence, RI
Builder – Highland Builders, Tiverton, RI
Landscape – Derek van Lent, Block Island, RI
Photography – Warren Jagger, Providence, RI

Danevic/Bernard House (2006)
Location – Block Island, Rhode Island
Structural Engineer – Yoder & Tidwell, LTD,
   Providence, RI
Builder – Highland Builders, Tiverton RI
Interiors – Mary Fran Brassard, Little Silver, NJ
Photography – Warren Jagger, Providence, RI

Stonington House (2005)
Location – Stonington, Connecticut
Structural Engineer – Yoder & Tidwell, LTD.,
   Providence, RI
Interiors – Oz Maille, Design Site, New York, NY
Builder – Robert D. Wood, Stonington, CT
Photography – Warren Jagger, Providence, RI

Contributors

The following people contributed to
the work in this book:

—

Gale Goff, *Senior Associate*
Ann Delmonico
Joseph Fenton
Joshua Fogg
Kevin Baker
Greg Maxwell
Robin Linhares
William Young
Michael Tyrwhitt-Drake
Scott Galczynski
Nick DePace
Glenn Buie
Carolyn Morgan

—

Nine outstanding clients

—

Two outstanding wives:
Darcy Magratten
Judith McClain